SHAKESPEARE'S
FLORA

SHAKESPEARE'S FLORA

First published in Great Britain in 1999 by
PAVILION BOOKS LIMITED
London House, Great Eastern Wharf
Parkgate Road, London SW11 4NQ

Illustrations © the bodleian library, oxford
Introduction © Jenny De Gex, 1995, 1999

text and pictures compiled by jenny de gex
Design and layout © Pavilion Books Ltd.

Designed by David Fordham

A CIP catalogue record for this book is available
from the British Library.

ISBN 1 86205 288 3

Printed in singapore by kyodo

2 4 6 8 10 9 7 5 3 1

This book can be ordered direct from the publisher. Please contact
the Marketing Department. But try your bookshop first.

Contents

ꞎNTRODUCTION

S HAKESPEARE's expert knowledge on a variety of sub-
jects and professions ranges effortlessly from science to
art, so it comes as no surprise to us that his sublime
words also include imagery of one of the growing fashions of
Tudor times, gardening. His observations of plants and the
beauties of nature stem, however, from his life as a countryman, not as a botanist. He was able to communicate the
simple pleasures of the scent or colours of flowers in a few
well-chosen words, bringing the plants to life in a fresh and
evocative manner.

Shakespeare speaks lovingly of flowers – in expressions
that are not merely poetical, but faithfully describing what
he daily observed – with obvious affection. 'fresh and fragrant flowers', 'the beauteous flowers', 'the sweet summer
buds', 'blossoms passing fair', 'the darling buds of May'.

The herbs, flowers and trees he describes, even when set
in fictitious countries such as 'Illyria', are all English plants
which, with few exceptions, might be seen in the hedgerows
or woods of Warwickshire, in his own or his friends' gardens.
The descriptions are vivid and tell of the countryside he
loved. He introduces many common flowers into his poems
and plays, but there are also some notable omissions, such as
snowdrop, forget-me-not, foxglove, lily-of-the-valley. Yet
violets are mentioned eighteen times, roses over a hundred.

In *A Midsummer Night's Dream* the pansy is the:

> *little western flower,–*
> *Before, milk-white, now purple with love's wound –*
> *And maidens call it love-in-idleness*

which is upon 'sleeping eyelids laid' to weave the magic spell, so central to the plot.

Wild flowers are gathered from their natural habitats – 'flat meads', 'turfy mountains', 'rose-banks', 'unshrubbed down' – but Shakespeare is equally at home in formal gardens with 'pleached bowers' and 'leafy orchards'. Much contemporary folklore, plantlore and herbal knowledge is contained in his colourful language, and also a familiarity with medical 'quackery' in the detailed description of an apothecary's shop in *Romeo and Juliet*.

Yet Shakespeare was neither a peasant nor a village lad, but from good middle-class stock, his father being one of the wealthier citizens of Stratford-upon-Avon. It is not known when he first appeared in London, although the story goes that he had to leave Stratford when caught poaching deer at nearby Charlecote Park. Records show that he became a successful dramatist sometime before 1592, and by 1594 he was a member of the Lord Chamberlain's company, which became the King's Company (of players) in 1603, writing many popular plays for them. He prospered and invested in property at Stratford, where he died in 1616.

In his plays he describes England as a 'sea-walled garden', and some twenty-nine scenes are set in gardens, where characters seek a moment's privacy – or conspiracy – to talk in private, or walk hand-in-hand. In the history plays discussions of national import are often set in gardens – notably with reference to the red and white roses of the houses of York and Lancaster, so fiercely fought over during the fifteenth century in the Wars of the Roses. The white rose was the emblem of the Plantagenet kings, the red of the

Tudors who replaced them, after fearsome battles and considerable treachery.

However, the strong rule of the Tudors ushered in a period of peace and prosperity for the Elizabethans, who were keen gardeners. Medieval garden enclosures expanded into stately 'pleasaunces', with 'curious knotted gardens', pleached alleys, bowling-greens, orchards, vineyards, summer bowers, fountains, dovecotes and beds planted in mixed colours.

Gardens as Shakespeare would have known them were uniform and formal, in every minute detail. Bacon's rule was that a 'garden is best to be square'. The garden was considered to be a continuation of the house, designed to harmonize with the architecture of the building. The square enclosure was bounded either by a high wall or hedge, preferably of hornbeam. Within this space the garden was laid out in formal shapes, with paths and alleys, lined with trees, dividing the square into four or more compartments. All of this was secondary to the great feature of Elizabethan gardens, the knot garden, formed of low hedges of rosemary, dwarf box, thrift or lavender. Sometimes these patterns were in the shape of heraldic beasts, although most surviving designs are abstract and geometric. Sometimes the pattern worked in living green was filled with coloured gravels, sometimes with flowering plants. Other areas of the garden had their own specific purposes: orchards for fruit, kitchen gardens for vegetables, separate gardens for herbs and salading. Salads were very popular, and flowers as well as herbs were often added as edible decoration. Thomas Tusser's book *Five Hundred Points of Good Husbandry*, first published in 1573, went through twelve editions during Elizabeth's reign: testimony to increased interest in gardens among ordinary people.

In 1548 William Turner, the founding father of English botany, published his *New Herball*. Exchanges of knowledge and plants from the Low Countries and Italy were now increasingly influential. Shakespeare was a near contemporary of John Gerard, gardener to Lord Burleigh, who lived from 1545 to 1612. Conjecture has been made that they were acquainted, and that Shakespeare may have seen Gerard's garden, where more than a thousand plants were grown, 'all manner of strange trees, herbes, rootes, plants, flowers and other such rare things'. Gerard published his own famous *Herball* in 1597, partly assembled from the writings of the Flemish botanist Rembert Dodoens, partly from his own observations, with 1,800 woodcut illustrations taken from German woodblocks. It remains a fascinating catalogue of Elizabethan plants and their 'vertues'.

The Elizabethan age, reflected in portraiture and decoration, as well as in verse and literature, shows a strong interest in flowers. Paintings often depict the subject with a flower in the hand, or tucked into a dress, or surrounded by roses. Plasterwork and emblems in books and needlework all represent flowers. Horticultural skills increased, improving flower colouring, increasing their size, or creating double flowers, with acknowledgement to the progress made by the Dutch.

The great houses – Hardwick, Longleat, Theobalds (where Gerard worked) – reflect the glory of this age.

The illustrations for this anthology have been chosen from a pattern book, perhaps for painted cloth or embroidery, dating from the early Tudor period. It is of uncertain origin, but probably East Anglian, being very similar to a rare contemporary manuscript from Helmingham Hall in Suffolk, known as the *Helmingham Herbal* (now in the Mellon Collection). Both give a remarkable picture of natural history in early Tudor times, together with domestic details.

Shakespeare was not only a keen observer of plants, but was also knowledgeable about the more practical side of gardening, often using this knowledge to ironical or dramatic effect, as illustrated by this allegorical extract from *Richard II*:

> O, *what pity is it,*
> *That he had not so trimm'd and dress'd this land*
> *As we this garden! We at time of year*
> *Do wound the bark, the skin of our fruit-trees,*
> *Lest, being over-proud in sap and blood,*
> *With too much riches it confound itself:*
> *Had he done so to great and growing men,*
> *They might have lived to hear and he to taste*
> *Their fruits of duty; superfluous branches*
> *We lop away, that bearing boughs may live:*
> *Had he done so, himself had borne the crown*
> *Which waste of idle hours hath quite thrown down.*

THE FLOWERS

KING HENRY VIII

ACT V   SCENE V

Cranmer:

This royal infant, (Heaven still move about her!)
Though in her cradle, yet now promises
Upon this land a thousand thousand blessings,
Which time shall bring to ripeness . . .

She shall be loved, and fear'd: her own shall bless her:
Her foes shake like a field of beaten corn,
And hang their heads with sorrow: good grows with
    her:
In her days every man shall eat in safety,
Under his own vine, what he plants; and sing
The merry songs of peace to all his neighbours:
God shall be truly known; and those about her
From her shall read the perfect ways of honour,
And by those claim their greatness, not by blood . . .

She shall be, to the happiness of England,
An agèd princess; many days shall see her,
And yet no day without a deed to crown it.
Would I had known no more! but she must die –
She must, the saints must have her – yet a virgin;
A most unspotted lily shall she pass
To the ground, and all the world shall mourn her.

THE ASPHODEL

A WINTER'S TALE

ACT IV   SCENE III

Perdita:

Now, my fairest friend,
I would I had some flowers o' the spring, that might
Become your time of day; and yours, and yours;
That wear upon your virgin branches yet
Your maidenheads growing: – O, Proserpina,
For the flowers now, that, frighted, thou lett'st fall
From Dis's waggon! daffodils,
That come before the swallow dares, and take
The winds of March with beauty; violets, dim,
But sweeter than the lids of Juno's eyes,
Or Cytherea's breath; pale primroses,
That die unmarried, ere they can behold
Bright Phœbus in his strength, a malady
Most incident to maids; bold oxlips, and
The crown-imperial; lilies of all kinds,
The flower-de-luce being one! Oh! these I lack,
To make you garlands of; and, my sweet friend,
To strew him o'er and o'er.

THE DAISY

LOVE'S LABOUR'S LOST

ACT V   SCENE II

S<small>ONG</small>

S<small>PRING</small>

I

When daisies pied, and violets blue,
 And lady-smocks all silver white,
And cuckoo-buds of yellow hue,
 Do paint the meadows with delight,
The cuckoo then, on every tree,
Mocks married men, for thus sings he,
    Cuckoo;
Cuckoo, cuckoo, – O word of fear,
Unpleasing to a married ear!

II

When shepherds pipe on oaten straws,
 And merry larks are ploughmen's clocks,
When turtles tread, and rooks, and daws,
 And maidens bleach their summer smocks,
The cuckoo then, on every tree,
Mocks married men, for thus sings he,
    Cuckoo;
Cuckoo, cuckoo, – O word of fear,
Unpleasing to a married ear!

THE STRAWBERRY

KING HENRY V

ACT I SCENE V

Ely:

The strawberry grows underneath the nettle;
And wholesome berries thrive and ripen best
Neighbour'd by fruit of baser quality:
And so the prince obscured his contemplation
Under the veil of wildness; which, no doubt,
Grew like the summer grass, fastest by night,
Unseen, yet crescive in his faculty.

Canterbury:

It must be so; for miracles are ceased;
And therefore we must needs admit the means
How things are perfected.

BROOM

ACT I SCENE I

Gonzalo:

Now would I give a thousand furlongs of sea for an acre of barren ground; ling, heath, broom, furze, anything. The wills above be done! but I would fain die a dry death.

THE POPPY

OTHELLO

ACT III   SCENE III

Iago:

I will in Cassio's lodging lose this napkin,
And let him find it. Trifles, light as air,
Are to the jealous confirmations strong
As proofs of holy writ. This may do something.
The Moor already changes with my poison:
Dangerous conceits are, in their natures, poisons,
Which, at the first, are scarce found to distaste;
But, with a little act upon the blood,
Burn like the mines of sulphur. — I did say so —
Look, where he comes! Not poppy, nor mandragora,
Nor all the drowsy syrups of the world,
Shall ever medicine thee to that sweet sleep
Which thou ow'dst yesterday.

THE TEMPEST

ACT V   SCENE I

Ariel:

Where the bee sucks, there suck I;
In a cowslip's bell I lie:
There I couch when owls do cry.
On the bat's back I do fly
After summer merrily.
Merrily, merrily, shall I live now,
Under the blossom that hangs on the bough.

THE COWSLIP

A MIDSUMMER NIGHT'S DREAM

ACT II   SCENE I

Puck:

How now, spirit! whither wander you?

Fairy:

Over hill, over dale,
 Thorough bush, thorough briar,
Over park, over pale,
 Thorough flood, thorough fire,
I do wander everywhere,
Swifter than the moon's sphere;
And I serve the fairy queen,
To dew her orbs upon the green:
The cowslips tall her pensioners be;
In their gold coats spots you see;
Those be rubies, fairy favours,
In those freckles live their savours:
I must go seek some dew-drops here,
And hang a pearl in every cowslip's ear.
Farewell, thou lob of spirits, I'll be gone;
Our queen and all her elves come here anon.

Camomile

KING HENRY IV, PART I

ACT II   SCENE IV

Falstaff:

Peace, good pint-pot; peace, good tickle-brain. – Harry, I do not only marvel where thou spendest thy time, but also how thou art accompanied: for though the camomile, the more it is trodden the faster it grows, yet youth, the more it is wasted the sooner it wears.

THE COLUMBINE

THE DAISY

HAMLET

ACT IV SCENE VII

Queen:

There is a willow grows aslant a brook,
That shows his hoar leaves in the glassy stream;
There, with fantastic garlands did she come,
Of crow-flowers, nettles, daisies, and long purples,
That liberal shepherds give a grosser name,
But our cold maids do dead men's fingers call them:
There, on the pendent boughs her coronet weeds
Clambering to hang, an envious sliver broke;
When down the weedy trophies, and herself,
Fell in the weeping brook. Her clothes spread wide;
And, mermaid-like, a while they bore her up:
Which time, she chanted snatches of old tunes;
As one incapable of her own distress,
Or like a creature native and indued
Unto that element: but long it could not be,
Till that her garments, heavy with their drink,
Pull'd the poor wretch from her melodious lay
To muddy death.

THE EGLANTINE

A MIDSUMMER NIGHT'S DREAM

ACT II   SCENE I

Oberon:

I know a bank where the wild thyme blows,
Where ox-lips and the nodding violet grows;
Quite over-canopied with luscious woodbine,
With sweet musk-roses, and with eglantine:
There sleeps Titania, sometime of the night,
Lull'd in these flowers with dances and delight;
And there the snake throws her enamell'd skin,
Weed wide enough to wrap a fairy in:
And with the juice of this I'll streak her eyes,
And make her full of hateful fantasies.
Take thou some of it, and seek through this grove:
A sweet Athenian lady is in love
With a disdainful youth: anoint his eyes;
But do it when the next thing he espies
May be the lady. Thou shalt know the man
By the Athenian garments he hath on.
Effect it with some care; that he may prove
More fond on her, than she upon her love:
And look thou meet me ere the first cock crow.

VETCH

THE TEMPEST

ACT IV   SCENE I

Iris:

Ceres, most bounteous lady, thy rich leas
Of wheat, rye, barley, vetches, oats, and pease;
Thy turfy mountains, where live nibbling sheep,
And flat meads thatch'd with stover, them to keep;
Thy banks with pioned and twilled brims,
Which spongy April at thy hest betrims,
To make cold nymphs chaste crowns; and thy broom
    groves,
Whose shadow the dismissed bachelor loves,
Being lass-lorn; thy pole-clipp'd vineyard;
And thy sea-marge steril, and rocky hard,
Where thou thyself dost air: the queen o' the sky,
Whose watery arch, and messenger, am I,
Bids thee leave these; and with her sovereign grace,
Here on this grass-plot, in this very place,
To come and sport: her peacocks fly amain:
Approach, rich Ceres, her to entertain.

THE VINE

ACT IV   SCENE I

Ceres:

Earth's increase, foison plenty,
Barns and garners never empty;
Vines with clustering bunches growing;
Plants with goodly burden bowing:
Spring come to you, at the farthest,
In the very end of harvest!
Scarcity and want shall shun you;
Ceres' blessing so is on you.

THE MARIGOLD

Let those who are in favour with their stars,
Of public honour and proud titles boast,
Whilst I, whom fortune of such triumph bars,
Unlook'd for joy in that I honour most.
Great princes' favourites their fair leaves spread
But as the marigold at the sun's eye;
And in themselves their pride lies burièd,
For at a frown they in their glory die.
The painful warrior famoused for fight,
After a thousand victories once foil'd,
Is from the book of honour razèd quite,
And all the rest forgot for which he toil'd:
    Then happy I, that love and am beloved
    Where I may not remove, nor be removed.

THE RAPE OF LUCRECE

Her lily hand her rosy cheek lies under,
Cozening the pillow of a lawful kiss;
Who, therefore angry, seems to part in sunder,
Swelling on either side to want his bliss;
Between whose hills her head entombed is:
　　Where, like a virtuous monument, she lies,
　　To be admired of lewd unhallow'd eyes.

Without the bed her other fair hand was,
On the green coverlet; whose perfect white
Show'd like an April daisy on the grass,
With pearly sweat, resembling dew of night.
Her eyes, like marigolds, had sheathed their light,
　　And canopied in darkness sweetly lay,
　　Till they might open to adorn the day.

Her hair, like golden threads, play'd with her
　　breath;
O modest wantons! wanton modesty!
Showing life's triumph in the map of death,
And death's dim look in life's mortality:
Each in her sleep themselves so beautify,
　　As if between them twain there were no strife,
　　But that life lived in death, and death in life.

THE DAFFODIL

A WINTER'S TALE

ACT IV   SCENE II

Autolycus:

When daffodils begin to peer,
    With heigh! the doxy over the dale,
Why then comes in the sweet o' the year;
    For the red blood reigns in the winter's pale.

The white sheet bleaching on the hedge,
    With heigh! the sweet birds, O, how they sing!
Doth set my pugging tooth on edge;
    For a quart of ale is a dish for a king.

The lark that tirra-lirra chants,
    With heigh! with heigh! the thrush and the jay:
Are summer songs for me and my aunts,
    While we lie tumbling in the hay.

ℭHE CARNATION

A WINTER'S TALE

ACT IV SCENE III

Perdita:

For you there's rosemary, and rue; these keep
Seeming, and savour, all the winter long:
Grace, and remembrance, be to you both,
And welcome to our shearing!

Polixenes:

Shepherdess,
(A fair one are you,) well you fit our ages
With flowers of winter.

Perdita:

Sir, the year growing ancient, —
Not yet on summer's death, nor on the birth
Of trembling winter, — the fairest flowers o' the season
Are our carnations, and streak'd gillyvors,
Which some call nature's bastards: of that kind
Our rustic garden's barren, and I care not
To get slips of them.

Hyssop

OTHELLO

ACT I   SCENE III

Iago:

Virtue? a fig! 'tis in ourselves that we are thus, or thus.
Our bodies are our gardens; to the which our wills are
gardeners: so that if we will plant nettles, or sow let-
tuce; set hyssop, and weed up thyme; supply it with
one gender of herbs, or distract it with many; either to
have it sterile with idleness, or manured with industry;
why, the power and corrigible authority of this lies in
our wills. If the balance of our lives had not one scale of
reason to poise another of sensuality, the blood and
baseness of our natures would conduct us to most pre-
posterous conclusions: but we have reason to cool our
raging motions, our carnal stings, our unbitted lusts;
whereof I take this, that you call love, to be a sect or
scion.

ROSEMARY

ROMEO AND JULIET

ACT IV SCENE V

Friar Laurence:

Peace, ho, for shame! confusion's cure lives not
In these confusions. Heaven and yourself
Had part in this fair maid; now Heaven hath all,
And all the better is it for the maid:
Your part in her you could not keep from death;
But Heaven keeps his part in eternal life.
The most you sought was – her promotion;
For 'twas your heaven, she should be advanced:
And weep ye now, seeing she is advanced,
Above the clouds, as high as heaven itself?
O, in this love, you love your child so ill,
That you run mad, seeing that she is well:
She's not well married that lives married long;
But she's best married that dies married young.
Dry up your tears, and stick your rosemary
On this fair corse; and, as the custom is,
In all her best array bear her to church:
For though some nature bids us all lament,
Yet nature's tears are reason's merriment,

THE LILY

THE PASSIONATE PILGRIM

Fair is my love, but not so fair as fickle;
Mild as a dove, but neither true nor trusty;
Brighter than glass, and yet, as glass is, brittle;
Softer than wax, and yet, as iron, rusty:
    A lily pale, with damask dye to grace her,
    None fairer, nor none falser to deface her.

Her lips to mine how often hath she join'd,
Between each kiss her oaths of true love swearing!
How many tales to please me hath she coin'd,
Dreading my love, the loss thereof still fearing!
    Yet in the midst of all her pure protestings,
    Her faith, her oaths, her tears, and all were jestings.

She burn'd with love, as straw with fire flameth,
She burn'd out love, as soon as straw outburneth,
She framed the love, and yet she foil'd the framing,
She bade love last, and yet she fell a-turning.
    Was this a lover, or a lecher whether?
    Bad in the best, though excellent in neither.

BELLADONNA

ROMEO AND JULIET

ACT II SCENE III

Friar Laurence:

The gray-eyed morn smiles on the frowning night,
Checkering the eastern clouds with streaks of light;
And flecked darkness like a drunkard reels
From forth day's path, and Titan's fiery wheels:
Now ere the sun advance his burning eye,
The day to cheer, and night's dank dew to dry,
I must up-fill this osier cage of ours,
With baleful weeds, and precious-juicèd flowers.
The earth, that's nature's mother, is her tomb;
What is her burying grave, that is her womb:
And from her womb children of divers kind
We sucking on her natural bosom find;
Many for many virtues excellent,
None but for some, and yet all different.
O, mickle is the powerful grace, that lies
In plants, herbs, stones, and their true qualities:
For nought so vile that on the earth doth live,
But to the earth some special good doth give;
Nor aught so good, but, strain'd from that fair use,

Revolts from true birth, stumbling on abuse.
Virtue itself turns vice, being misapplied;
And vice sometime's by action dignified.
Within the infant rind of this weak flower
Poison hath residence, and medicine power:
For this, being smelt, with that part cheers each part;
Being tasted, slays all senses with the heart.
Two such opposèd kings encamp them still
In man as well as herbs, – grace, and rude will;
And, where the worser is predominant,
Full soon the canker death eats up that plant.

THE VIOLET

TWELFTH NIGHT; OR, WHAT YOU WILL

ACT I   SCENE I

Orsino, Duke of Illyria:

If music be the food of love, play on;
Give me excess of it; that, surfeiting,
The appetite may sicken, and so die. –
That strain again! – it had a dying fall:
Oh, it came o'er my ear like the sweet sound
That breathes upon a bank of violets,
Stealing and giving odour! – Enough; no more;
'Tis not so sweet now, as it was before.
O spirit of love, how quick and fresh art thou!
That notwithstanding thy capacity
Receiveth as the sea, nought enters there,
Of what validity and pitch soever,
But falls into abatement and low price,
Even in a minute! so full of shapes is fancy,
That it alone is high-fantastical.

PERICLES

ACT IV   SCENE I

Marina:

No: I will rob Tellus of her weed,
To strew thy green with flowers: the yellows, blues,
The purple violets, and marigolds,
Shall as a carpet hang upon thy grave,
While summer days do last. Ah me! poor maid,
Born in a tempest, when my mother died,
This world to me is like a lasting storm,
Whirring me from my friends.

THE VIOLET

The forward violet thus did I chide:
  Sweet thief, whence didst thou steal thy sweet that
    smells,
  If not from my love's breath? The purple pride
  Which on thy soft cheek for complexion dwells
  In my love's veins thou hast too grossly dyed.
  The lily I condemned for thy hand,
  And buds of marjoram had stol'n thy hair;
  The roses fearfully on thorns did stand,
  One blushing shame, another white despair;
  A third, nor red nor white, had stol'n of both,
  And to his robbery had annex'd thy breath;
  But, for his theft, in pride of all his growth
  A vengeful canker eat him up to death.
    More flowers I noted, yet I none could see
    But sweet or colour it had stol'n from thee.

ℳINT

A WINTER'S TALE

ACT IV   SCENE III

Perdita:

Here's flowers for you;
Hot lavender, mints, savory, marjoram;
The marigold, that goes to bed with the sun,
And with him rises weeping; these are flowers
Of middle summer, and, I think, they are given
To men of middle age: you are very welcome.

RUSHES

ACT III   SCENE I

Owen Glendower:

She bids you on the wanton rushes lay you down,
And rest your gentle head upon her lap,
And she will sing the song that pleaseth you,
And on your eyelids crown the god of sleep,
Charming your blood with pleasing heaviness;
Making such difference betwixt wake and sleep,
As is the difference betwixt day and night,
The hour before the heavenly-harness'd team
Begins his golden progress in the east.

Mortimer:

With all my heart I'll sit and hear her sing:
By that time will our book, I think, be drawn.

Glendower:

Do so;
And those musicians that shall play to you,
Hang in the air a thousand leagues from hence;
And straight they shall be here: sit, and attend.

44

GARLIC

A MIDSUMMER NIGHT'S DREAM

ACT IV SCENE II

Bottom:

Not a word of me. All that I will tell you is, that the duke hath dined: – get your apparel together; good strings to your beards, new ribbons to your pumps; meet presently at the palace; every man look o'er his part; for, the short and the long is, our play is pre-ferred. In any case, let Thisby have clean linen: and let not him that plays the lion pare his nails, for they shall hang out for the lion's claws. And, most dear actors, eat no onions, nor garlic, for we are to utter sweet breath; and I do not doubt but to hear them say it is a sweet comedy. No more words; away; go, away

THE PANSY

ACT II SCENE I

Oberon:

That very time I saw, (but thou couldst not,)
Flying between the cold moon and the earth,
Cupid all arm'd: a certain aim he took
At a fair vestal, thronèd by the west;
And loosed his love-shaft smartly from his bow,
As it should pierce a hundred thousand hearts:
But I might see young Cupid's fiery shaft
Quench'd in the chaste beams of the watery moon;
And the imperial votaress passed on,
In maiden meditation, fancy-free.
Yet mark'd I where the bolt of Cupid fell:
It fell upon a little western flower, –
Before, milk-white, now purple with love's wound –
And maidens call it love-in-idleness.
Fetch me that flower: the herb I show'd thee once;
The juice of it on sleeping eyelids laid,
Will make or man or woman madly dote
Upon the next live creature that it sees.
Fetch me this herb: and be thou here again,
Ere the leviathan can swim a league.

Puck:

I'll put a girdle round about the earth
In forty minutes.

Oberon:

Having once this juice,
I'll watch Titania when she is asleep,
And drop the liquor of it in her eyes:
The next thing then she waking looks upon,
(Be it on lion, bear, or wolf, or bull,
On meddling monkey, or on busy ape,)
She shall pursue it with the soul of love.
And ere I take this charm off from her sight,
(As I can take it, with another herb,)
I'll make her render up her page to me.
But who comes here? I am invisible;
And I will overhear their conference.

ACT III   SCENE II

Oberon:

Then crush this herb into Lysander's eye,
Whose liquor hath this virtuous property,
To take from thence all error, with his might,
And make his eyeballs roll with wonted sight.
When they next wake, all this derision
Shall seem a dream, and fruitless vision;
And back to Athens shall the lovers wend,
With league, whose date till death shall never end.
Whiles I in this affair do thee employ,
I'll to my queen, and beg her Indian boy;
And then I will her charmed eye release
From monster's view, and all things shall be peace.

THE ROSE

O how much more doth beauty beauteous seem,
By that sweet ornament which truth doth give!
The rose looks fair, but fairer we it deem
For that sweet odour which doth in it live.
The canker-blooms have full as deep a dye
As the perfumèd tincture of the roses,
Hang on such thorns, and play as wantonly
When summer's breath their masked buds discloses;
But, for their virtue only is their show,
They live unwoo'd, and unrespected fade;
Die to themselves. Sweet roses do not so;
Of their sweet deaths are sweetest odours made:
   And so of you, beauteous and lovely youth,
    When that shall fade, by verse distils your truth.

THE FOXGLOVE

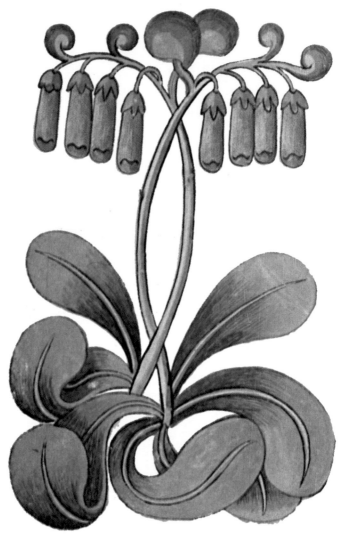

THE BLACKBERRY

AS YOU LIKE IT

ACT III   SCENE II

Rosalind:

No; I will not cast away my physic but on those that are sick. There is a man haunts the forest that abuses our young plants with carving *Rosalind* on their barks; hangs odes upon hawthorns, and elegies on brambles; all, forsooth, deifying the name of Rosalind: if I could meet that fancy-monger I would give him some good counsel, for he seems to have the quotidian of love upon him.

Orlando:

I am he that is so love-shaked; I pray you, tell me your remedy.

Rosalind:

There is none of my uncle's marks upon you: he taught me how to know a man in love; in which cage of rushes, I am sure, you are not prisoner.

THE OAK

ACT II   SCENE I

Puck:

The king doth keep his revels here tonight;
Take heed, the queen come not within his sight,
For Oberon is passing fell and wrath,
Because that she, as her attendant, hath
A lovely boy stolen from an Indian king;
She never had so sweet a changeling:
And jealous Oberon would have the child
Knight of his train, to trace the forests wild:
But she, perforce, withholds the lovèd boy
Crowns him with flowers, and makes him all her joy:
And now they never meet in grove, or green,
By fountain clear, or spangled starlight sheen,
But they do square; that all their elves, for fear,
Creep into acorn-cups, and hide them there.

Rue

ACT IV   SCENE V

Ophelia:

There's rosemary, that's for remembrance; *pray, love, remember*: and there is pansies, that's for thoughts.

Laertes:

A document in madness; thoughts and remembrance fitted.

Ophelia:

There's fennel for you, and columbines: – there's rue for you; and here's some for me: – we may call it herb of grace o'Sundays: – oh, you must wear your rue with a difference. – There's a daisy: – I would give you some violets, but they withered all, when my father died: – they say, he made a good end. –

THE POMEGRANATE

ROMEO AND JULIET

ACT III   SCENE V

Juliet:

Wilt thou be gone? it is not yet near day:
It was the nightingale, and not the lark,
That pierced the fearful hollow of thine ear;
Nightly she sings on yon pomegranate-tree:
Believe me, love, it was the nightingale.

Romeo:

It was the lark, the herald of the morn,
No nightingale: look, love, what envious streaks
Do lace the severing clouds in yonder east:
Night's candles are burnt out, and jocund day
Stands tiptoe on the misty mountain tops;
I must be gone and live, or stay and die.

Juliet:

Yon light is not daylight, I know it, I:
It is some meteor that the sun exhales,
To be to thee this night a torch-bearer,
And light thee on thy way to Mantua:
Therefore stay yet, thou need'st not to be gone.

THE MULBERRY

A MIDSUMMER NIGHT'S DREAM

ACT III   SCENE I

Titania:

Be kind and courteous to this gentleman;
Hop in his walks, and gambol in his eyes;
Feed him with apricocks, and dewberries;
With purple grapes, green figs, and mulberries;
The honey-bags steal from the humble-bees,
And, for night-tapers, crop their waxen thighs,
And light them at the fiery glow-worm's eyes,
To have my love to bed, and to arise;
And pluck the wings from painted butterflies,
To fan the moonbeams from his sleeping eyes:
Nod to him, elves, and do him courtesies.

ℭHE CHERRY

A MIDSUMMER NIGHT'S DREAM

ACT III   SCENE II

Helena:

We, Hermia, like two artificial gods,
Have with our needles created both one flower,
Both on one sampler, sitting on one cushion,
Both warbling of one song, both in one key;
As if our hands, our sides, voices, and minds,
Had been incorporate. So we grew together,
Like to a double cherry, seeming parted;
But yet a union in partition,
Two lovely berries moulded on one stem:
So, with two seeming bodies, but one heart,
Two of the first, like coats in heraldry,
Due but to one, and crowned with one crest.
And will you rent our ancient love asunder,
To join with men in scorning your poor friend?
It is not friendly, 'tis not maidenly:
Our sex, as well as I, may chide you for it;
Though I alone do feel the injury.

CLOVER

KING HENRY V

ACT V   SCENE II

Duke of Burgundy:

My duty to you both, on equal love,
Great kings of France and England! That I have
    labour'd
With all my wits, my pains, and strong
    endeavours,
To bring your most imperial majesties
Unto this bar and royal interview,
Your mightiness on both parts best can witness.
Since then my office hath so far prevail'd
That face to face, and royal eye to eye,
You have congreeted; let it not disgrace me,
If I demand, before this royal view,
What rub, or what impediment, there is,
Why that the naked, poor, and mangled peace,
Dear nurse of arts, plenties, and joyful births,
Should not, in this best garden of the world,
Our fertile France, put up her lovely visage?
Alas! she hath from France too long been chased;
And all her husbandry doth lie on heaps,
Corrupting in its own fertility.
Her vine, the merry cheerer of the heart,
Unprunèd dies: her hedges even-pleach'd,
Like prisoners wildly overgrown with hair,
Put forth disorder'd twigs: her fallow leas
The darnel, hemlock, and rank fumitory,
Doth root upon; while that the coulter rusts,
That should deracinate such savagery:
The even mead, that erst brought sweetly forth
The freckled cowslip, burnet, and green clover,

58

Wanting the scythe, all uncorrected, rank,
Conceives by idleness; and nothing teems
But hateful docks, rough thistles, kecksies, burs,
Losing both beauty and utility:
And as our vineyards, fallows, meads, and
    hedges,
Defective in their natures, grow to wildness,
Even so our houses, and ourselves, and children,
Have lost, or do not learn, for want of time,
The sciences that should become our country;
But grow like savages, – as soldiers will,
That nothing do but meditate on blood, –
To swearing, and stern looks, diffused attire,
And everything that seems unnatural.
Which to reduce into our former favour
You are assembled; and my speech entreats
That I may know the let, why gentle peace
Should not expel these inconveniences,
And bless us with her former qualities.

THE ROSE

My mistress' eyes are nothing like the sun;
Coral is far more red than her lips' red:
If snow be white, why then her breasts are dun;
If hairs be wires, black wires grow on her head.
I have seen roses damask'd, red and white,
But no such roses see I in her cheeks;
And in some perfumes is there more delight
Than in the breath that from my mistress reeks.
I love to hear her speak, – yet well I know
That music hath a far more pleasing sound;
I grant I never saw a goddess go, –
My mistress, when she walks, treads on the
        ground;
    And yet, by heaven, I think my love as rare
    As any she belied with false compare.

THE THISTLE

OUR SEA-WALLED GARDEN

KING RICHARD II

ACT III   SCENE IV

Gardener:

Go, bind thou up yon' dangling apricocks,
Which, like unruly children, make their sire
Stoop with oppression of their prodigal weight:
Give some supportance to the bending twigs.
Go thou, and, like an executioner,
Cut off the heads of too-fast-growing sprays,
That look too lofty in our commonwealth:
All must be even in our government.
You thus employ'd, I will go root away
The noisome weeds, that without profit suck
The soil's fertility from wholesome flowers.

Servant:

Why should we, in the compass of a pale,
Keep law, and form, and due proportion,
Showing, as in a model, our firm estate,
When our sea-walled garden, the whole land,
Is full of weeds; her fairest flowers choked up,
Her fruit-trees all unpruned, her hedges ruin'd,
Her knots disorder'd, and her wholesome herbs
Swarming with caterpillars?

Picture Credits

All flower illustrations are details taken from the
MS Ashmole 1504, reproduced by courtesy
of the Bodleian Library, Oxford
except for the following:

p.6: Double purple hollihocke from John Gerarde's
Herball, 1957 (Royal Horticultural Society,
Lindley library, London)

p.7: Gateway to an Elizabethan herb garden from
Cats' *Emblems*, 1622

p.9 Title page of Hans Sibmacher's *Neues Modelbuch*, 1604

p.12 Elizabeth I by Nicholas Hilliard
(Courtesy of the Board of Trustees of the
Victoria & Albert Museum, London)

SHAKESPEARE'S
FLORA & FAUNA

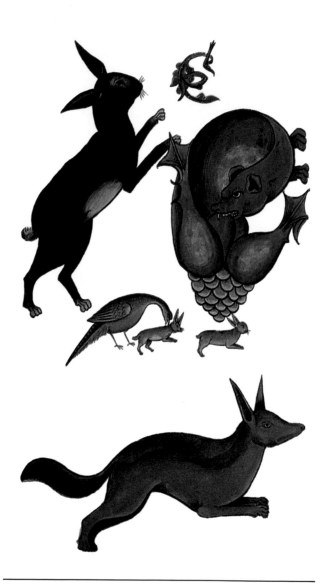

SHAKESPEARE'S FAUNA

Contents

ᴊNTRODUCTION

S HAKESPEARE uses no fewer than 4,000 allusions to animals in his character portrayals, and so this small anthology can serve only as a brief appetiser to further riches in the tradition of comparing animal and human characteristics.

There are several realms within this tradition, the first being the supernatural, where animals are gods or demons, or weird metamorphosed creatures. The second realm is that of the *un*natural – the jointless elephant, the fire-eating salamander, the unlicked bear cub, and the basilisk or cockatrice, whose fatal eye brought certain death. The third realm is the analogy between man and animals.

The study of physiognomy judged men by the alleged attributes of the animals they supposedly resembled physically. Shakespeare may have known Della Porta's work *De Humana Physiogonomonia*, which was a compilation taken from Aristotle's *Historia Animalium*. *Aesop's Fables* would have been familiar to an Elizabethan audience, as the European edition was circulated in the fifteenth century. The Aesopic tradition, going back to earlier mythology (whether of Greek or Indian origin), represents another aspect of animal analogy, as the *Fables* tell of the follies and foibles of men depicted behind animal masks. Aesop was on the school curriculum in Elizabethan times, and probably no school child escaped the teaching of 'morality' by these picturesque examples. Ovid's *Metamorphoses*, with which Shakespeare would also have been familiar, is a storehouse of animal gods, auguries and charms, compiled from oral and written traditions originating with primitive peoples and passed on through the civilizations of Egypt, the Orient and Greece. Later books on witchcraft and magic continued these age-old folk beliefs.

Shakespeare was a countryman born and bred in Warwickshire, and his first-hand observations of nature form strong elements throughout his plays and poetry. The changing moods of the seasons echo romance or tragedy; bird songs convey blissful harmony or act as dire warnings; creatures act as symbols or premonitions of evil deeds.

Although Shakespeare would have recognized domestic and farm animals, and hunted or indeed poached wild deer, he would only ever have known the more exotic animals from the limited knowledge available in the late sixteenth century, for he would have had no opportunity of observing them in their wild and natural state. A strange lore grew out of man's interest in animals as marvellous specimens of nature. Travellers' tales, such as Hakluyt's voyages or Marco Polo's earlier journeys, filled the imagination long before the advent of the more exact science of zoology. Not all the tales of monsters were entirely without foundation, and as the world became better known, their existence was proven by eye-witness accounts and drawings, or by skins and bones brought back from distant lands.

Legends of dragons, mermaids and unicorns abounded and were repeated in the few early encylopaedic works before the advent of scientific proof. None more so than that of the unicorn, whose horn was imbued with miraculous properties. Even though we now know that the horn comes from a small Arctic whale, the narwhal, its associations conjure up a strangely magical world. The origins of the myth are complex and buried deep in history: the unicorn's horn was once a pagan symbol of male fertility, but was later purified by the Christian church as a symbol of the Virgin's mystic impregnation.

Strange beliefs about animals were disseminated in works such as the first encyclopaedia, *De Proprietatibus Rerum* (Of the Properties of Things), written by Bartholomaeus Anglicus in the thirteenth century, and in the works of Albertus Magnus. The *Hortus Sanitatis* (or Medieval Health Handbook), famous for its herb lore, has a section on animal lore. Classical literature in translation, such as Pliny's *Historia Naturalis*, would also have been known to Shakespeare. Extraordinary remedies are described — for instance, 'the soles of the feet anointed with the fat of a Dormouse doth procure sleep.' So it is not a great leap from this to the strange concoctions of the witches' terrible brew in *Macbeth*, for magic and folklore were integral parts of everyday life.

Shakespeare combined these elements, stories from the classics, travel yarns, folklore, magic, childhood memories and heraldry, and used the old technique of animal analogy more extensively than any previous epic writers, dramatists or poets. Homer pictured warriors fighting like lions, boars and fierce bulls in the ferocity of war, and Shakespeare followed this technique.

Animal comparisons range from the bee to the lion, the former in a detailed description of an ideal kingdom modelled after the government of bees (*King Henry V*, Act I, Scene II); the latter, the 'king of beasts' in many of the history plays, where the English lion is at war with the French. The comparisons, used in so many different contexts — be they political, heroic, farcical, tragic, romantic or blatantly sexual — often typified the disposition, rather than appearance, of a character. Frequently they were used with hostile intent, as in metaphors of battle and treachery, or for censure or ridicule, in the case of villains (such as Richard III

Elephas hic per   Europam vifus eft
Anno 1629

or Shylock) and buffoons (such as Dogberry or Bottom). Richard III, whose brutish nature retains a certain majesty, is characterized as wolf, spider, tiger, boar and bloody dog. Armies rallied against 'the wretched, bloody and usurping boar', of whom it was said: 'never hung poison on a fouler toad'. His birth was heralded thus:

> *A cockatrice hast thou hatch'd to the world,*
> *Whose unavoided eye is murderous!*

Specific animals, such as the serpent, the fox and the wolf are associated with treachery and villainy. This can vary according to the context – a lion may alternately be cruel and merciful, an ape sensual and ludicrous. The word 'serpent' applied to Goneril means treacherous, as she struck 'with her tongue, most serpent-like upon the very heart'

(both she and Richard III are described as 'gilded serpents'),
but when applied to Cleopatra it means alluring and sen-
suous, Antony's 'serpent of old Nile'.

Gentler creatures like the lamb, dove, hare and birds convey expressions of love and friendship, or serve as innocent
victims, as for Katherine in *The Taming of the Shrew*: 'Tut!
She's a lamb, a dove, a fool to him.' One of the most pitiful
speeches from *Macbeth* comes when Macduff hears with
horror of the murder of his wife and children:

> *What! all my pretty chickens and their dam*
> *At one fell swoop?*

And Sir Andrew Aguecheek, one of the greatest fools in all
Shakespeare's work, is compared to witless animals, for his
'dormouse valour' and having 'not so much blood in his liver
as will clog the foot of a flea'.

Names are frequently used for the sake of word-play –
deer and dear, hart and heart – or for the double meaning
and innuendo conveyed by certain creatures. The Elizabethans had a bawdy sense of humour, and many of the animal
interpretations had a sexual meaning that is lost from our
current language. Where men and women abandon themselves to passion, they become beasts. Thus in *Othello*, Iago
describes how 'your daughter and the Moor are now making
the beast with two backs'. Although an ass was also a general
term of abuse, and Dogberry a quite natural ass, its other
meaning was not lost on Shakespearean audiences.

Like Aesop, Shakespeare often adopted a moral tone and
does not merely give us narrative: instead, he puts a moral or
political lesson into the words of his characters. In his por-
trayal of Mankind, he often makes sweeping generalizations,
turning to the animal kingdom for comparisons. He satirizes
or praises where appropriate the weak, villainous, pathetic
or heroic. The metamorphosis of man into animal often retains a human soul. In the words of Hamlet:

INTRODUCTION

> *What a piece of work is a man! How noble in*
> *reason! how infinite in faculty! in form and moving*
> *how express and admirable! in action how like an*
> *angel! in apprehension how like a god! the beauty*
> *of the world! the paragon of animals!*

Elizabethan staging, which used partial disguise of men as
animals, was violently condemned for 'metamorphosing
humane shape into bestiall forme'! Many supernatural
animal figures move across the Elizabethan stage: satyrs, har-
pies, animal familiars. The strangest, part-animal supernatural figure is Caliban – 'a freckled whelp, hag-born'.

> *What have we here? a man or a fish?*
> *Half a fish and half a monster.*

The illustrations for this anthology form part of a pattern
book dating from the early Tudor period, of uncertain origin
but similar to a rare contemporary manuscript from Suffolk
now in the Mellon Collection, known as the *Helmingham*
Herbal and Bestiary. Both works give a unique view of daily
life at the turn of the fifteenth century, and two strands can
be traced, as with Shakespeare: the moralistic, represented
by the bestiary; and the informative, mainly about hunting.
Legendary nature influenced the drawings, as did the styl-
ization of the new discipline of heraldry. The manuscripts
may have been patterns for textiles or embroidery.

The Elizabethans would have been closer to the Aesopic
traditions and to those of animal physiognomy than we are
today, but through Shakespeare's interpretations and
character portrayals we are made to see Man's fundamental
sensuality, stupidity and cruelty. Our passions and be-
haviour, at a basic level, are similar to those of all other
animals. It is only through the refinements of our civiliza-
tion, such as the richness of Shakespeare's language which
has endured for nearly 400 years, that we can rise above
these baser instincts.

THE APE

A MIDSUMMER NIGHT'S DREAM

ACT II   SCENE I

Oberon:

Having once this juice,
I'll watch Titania when she is asleep,
And drop the liquor of it in her eyes:
The next thing then she waking looks upon,
(Be it on lion, bear, or wolf, or bull,
On meddling monkey, or on busy ape,)
She shall pursue it with the soul of love.
And ere I take this charm off from her sight,
(As I can take it, with another herb,)
I'll make her render up her page to me.
But who comes here? I am invisible;
And I will overhear their conference.

THE BEAR

ACT III   SCENE IV

Lear:

Thou think'st 'tis much, that this contentious storm
Invades us to the skin: so 'tis to thee;
But where the greater malady is fix'd,
The lesser is scarce felt. Thou'dst shun a bear:
But if thy flight lay toward the roaring sea,
Thou'dst meet the bear i' the mouth. When the
        mind's free,
The body's delicate: the tempest in my mind
Doth from my senses take all feeling else,
Save what beats there. – Filial ingratitude!
Is it not as this mouth should tear this hand,
For lifting food to't? – But I will punish home: –
No, I will weep no more. – In such a night
To shut me out! – Pour on; I will endure: –
In such a night as this! O Regan, Goneril! –
Your old kind father, whose frank heart gave all, –
O, that way madness lies; let me shun that;
No more of that. –

THE BEAR

A MIDSUMMER NIGHT'S DREAM

ACT II SCENE II

Oberon:

What thou see'st, when thou dost wake,
(*Squeezes the flower on* TITANIA'*s eyelids*)
Do it for thy true-love take;
Love and languish for his sake;
Be it ounce, or cat, or bear,
Pard, or boar with bristled hair,
In thy eye that shall appear
When thou wak'st, it is thy dear;
Wake, when some vile thing is near.

THE BIRDS

VENUS AND ADONIS

'To see his face the lion walk'd along
Behind some hedge, because he would not fear him;
To recreate himself, when he hath sung,
The tiger would be tame, and gently hear him;
　If he had spoke, the wolf would leave his prey,
　And never fright the silly lamb that day.

'When he beheld his shadow in the brook,
The fishes spread on it their golden gills;
When he was by, the birds such pleasure took,
That some would sing, some other in their bills
　Would bring him mulberries, and ripe-red
　　cherries;
　He fed them with his sight, they him with
　　berries.'

THE CAT

PERICLES

ACT III   GOWER

Gower:

Now sleep yslaked hath the rout;
No din but snores, the house about,
Made louder by the o'er-fed breast
Of this most pompous marriage-feast,
The cat, with eyne of burning coal,
Now couches from the mouse's hole;
And crickets sing at the oven's mouth,
Aye the blither for their drouth.
Hymen hath brought the bride to bed,
Where, by the loss of maidenhead,
A babe is moulded. – Be attent,
And time that is so briefly spent,
With your fine fancies quaintly eche;
What's dumb in show, I'll plain with speech.

THE CAT

MACBETH

ACT IV   SCENE I

First Witch:

Thrice the brinded cat hath mew'd.
Second Witch: Thrice; and once the hedge-pig
   whined.
Third Witch: Harpier cries: – 'tis time, 'tis time.
First Witch: Round about the cauldron go;
In the poison'd entrails throw.

THE CAT

Toad, that under cold stone,
Days and nights hast thirty-one,
Swelter'd venom sleeping got,
Boil thou first i' the charmed pot!
All: Double, double toil and trouble;
Fire, burn; and, cauldron, bubble.
Second Witch: Fillet of a fenny snake,
In the cauldron boil and bake:
Eye of newt, and toe of frog,
Wool of bat, and tongue of dog,
Adder's fork, and blind-worm's sting,
Lizard's leg, and owlet's wing,
For a charm of powerful trouble,
Like a hell-broth boil and bubble.
All: Double, double toil and trouble;
Fire, burn; and, cauldron, bubble.
Third Witch: Scale of dragon, tooth of wolf;
Witches' mummy; maw, and gulf,
Of the ravin'd salt-sea shark;
Root of hemlock, digg'd i' the dark;
Liver of blaspheming Jew;
Gall of goat, and slips of yew,
Sliver'd in the moon's eclipse;
Nose of Turk, and Tartar's lips;
Finger of birth-strangled babe,
Ditch-deliver'd by a drab, –
Make the gruel thick and slab
Add thereto a tiger's chaudron,
For the ingredients of our cauldron.
All: Double, double toil and trouble;
Fire, burn; and, cauldron, bubble.
Second Witch: Cool it with a baboon's blood,
Then the charm is firm and good.

THE COCKATRICE

THE RAPE OF LUCRECE

Then, for thy husband and thy children's sake,
Tender my suit: bequeath not to their lot
The shame that from them no device can take,
The blemish that will never be forgot;
Worse than a slavish wipe, or birth-hour's blot:
   For marks descried in men's nativity
   Are nature's faults, not their own infamy.'

Here with a cockatrice' dead-killing eye
He rouseth up himself, and makes a pause;
While she, the picture of pure piety,
Like a white hind under the grype's sharp claws,
Pleads, in a wilderness, where are no laws,
   To the rough beast that knows no gentle right,
   Nor aught obeys but his foul appetite.

But when a black-faced cloud the world doth threat,
In his dim mist the aspiring mountains hiding,
From earth's dark womb some gentle gust doth get,
Which blows these pitchy vapours from their
    biding,
Hindering their present fall by this dividing;
   So his unhallow'd haste her words delays,
   And moody Pluto winks while Orpheus plays.

THE CROCODILE

OTHELLO

ACT IV   SCENE I

Desdemona:

I have not deserved this.

Lodovico:

My lord, this would not be believed in Venice,
Though I should swear I saw't: 'tis very much;
Make her amends; she weeps.

Othello:

O devil, devil!
If that the earth could teem with woman's tears,
Each drop she falls would prove a crocodile: –
Out of my sight!

Desdemona:

I will not stay to offend you.

THE DEER

VENUS AND ADONIS

'Fondling,' she saith, 'since I have hemm'd thee here,
Within the circuit of this ivory pale,
I'll be a park, and thou shalt be my deer;
Feed where thou wilt, on mountain or in dale:
  Graze on my lips; and if those hills be dry,
  Stray lower, where the pleasant fountains lie.

'Within this limit is relief enough,
Sweet bottom-grass, and high delightful plain,
Round rising hillocks, brakes obscure and rough,
To shelter thee from tempest and from rain;
  Then be my deer, since I am such a park;
  No dog shall rouse thee, though a thousand bark.'

THE DEER

VENUS AND ADONIS

And as she runs, the bushes in the way
Some catch her by the neck, some kiss her face,
Some twine about her thigh to make her stay;
She wildly breaketh from their strict embrace,
   Like a milch doe, whose swelling dugs do ache,
   Hasting to feed her fawn hid in some brake.

By this, she hears the hounds are at a bay;
Whereat she starts, like one that spies an adder
Wreathed up in fatal folds, just in his way,
The fear whereof doth make him shake and
      shudder;
   Even so the timorous yelping of the hounds
   Appals her senses, and her spirit confounds.

For now she knows it is no gentle chase,
But the blunt boar, rough bear, or lion proud,
Because the cry remaineth in one place,
Where fearfully the dogs exlaim aloud:
   Finding their enemy to be so curst,
   They all strain court'sy who shall cope him first.

This dismal cry rings sadly in her ear,
Through which it enters to surprise her heart;
Who, overcome by doubt and bloodless fear,
With cold-pale weakness numbs each feeling part:
   Like soldiers, when their captain once doth yield,
   They basely fly, and dare not stay the field.

THE DOG

MACBETH

ACT III   SCENE I

First Murderer:

We are men, my liege.

Macbeth:

Ay, in the catalogue ye go for men;
As hounds, and greyhounds, mongrels, spaniels, curs,
Shoughs, water-rugs, and demi-wolves, are cleped
All by the name of dogs: the valued file
Distinguishes the swift, the slow, the subtle,
The housekeeper, the hunter, every one
According to the gift which bounteous nature
Hath in him closed; whereby he does receive
Particular addition, from the bill
That writes them all alike: and so of men.
Now, if you have a station in the file,
Not in the worst rank of manhood, say it;
And I will put that business in your bosoms
Whose execution takes your enemy off;
Grapples you to the heart and love of us,
Who wear our health but sickly in his life,
Which in his death were perfect.

THE DOG

KING LEAR

ACT III   SCENE VI

Edgar:

Avaunt, you curs!
  Be thy mouth or black or white,
  Tooth that poisons if it bite;
  Mastiff, grey-hound, mongrel grim,
  Hound or spaniel, brach or lym;
  Or bobtail tike, or trundle-tail;
  Tom will make him weep and wail:
  For, with throwing thus my head,
  Dogs leap the hatch, and all are fled.

THE DOG

THE MERCHANT OF VENICE

ACT I   SCENE III

Shylock:

Signior Antonio, many a time and oft
In the Rialto you have rated me
About my moneys, and my usances:
Still have I borne it with a patient shrug;
For sufferance is the badge of all our tribe:
You call me misbeliever, cut-throat dog,
And spit upon my Jewish gaberdine,
And all for use of that which is mine own.
Well then, it now appears you need my help:
Go to, then: you come to me, and you say,
Shylock, we would have moneys; you say so;
You, that did void your rheum upon my beard,
And foot me, as you spurn a stranger cur
Over your threshold; moneys is your suit.
What should I say to you? Should I not say,
Hath a dog money? is it possible
A cur can lend three thousand ducats? or
Shall I bend low, and in a bondman's key,
With 'bated breath, and whispering humbleness,
Say this, –
Fair sir, you spet on me on Wednesday last;
You spurn'd me such a day; another time
You call'd me dog; and for these courtesies
I'll lend you thus much moneys?

THE DOG

JULIUS CAESAR

ACT III   SCENE I

Antony:

O pardon me, thou bleeding piece of earth,
That I am meek and gentle with these butchers!
Thou are the ruins of the noblest man
That ever livèd in the tide of times.
Woe to the hand that shed this costly blood!
Over thy wounds now do I prophesy, –
Which, like dumb mouths, do ope their ruby lips,
To beg the voice and utterance of my tongue, –
A curse shall light upon the limbs of men;
Domestic fury, and fierce civil strife,
Shall cumber all the parts of Italy:
Blood and destruction shall be so in use,
And dreadful objects so familiar,
That mothers shall but smile when they behold
Their infants quarter'd with the hands of war;
All pity choked with custom of fell deeds:
And Caesar's spirit, ranging for revenge,
With Até by his side, come hot from hell,
Shall in these confines, with a monarch's voice,
Cry *Havoc*, and let slip the dogs of war;
That this foul deed shall smell above the earth
With carrion men, groaning for burial.

THE DOLPHIN

ANTONY AND CLEOPATRA

ACT V   SCENE II

Cleopatra:

His legs bestrid the ocean: his rear'd arm
Crested the world: his voice was propertied
As all the tunèd spheres, and that to friends;
But when he meant to quail and shake the orb,
He was as rattling thunder. For his bounty,
There was no winter in't: an autumn 'twas,
That grew the more by reaping: his delights
Were dolphin-like; they show'd his back above
The element they lived in: in his livery
Walk'd crowns and crownets; realms and islands were
As plates dropp'd from his pocket.

Dolabella:

Cleopatra, –

Cleopatra:

Think you there was, or might be, such a man
As this I dreamt of?

Dolabella:

Gentle madam, no.

Cleopatra:

You lie, up to the hearing of the gods.
But, if there be, or ever were, one such,
It's past the size of dreaming: Nature wants stuff
To vie strange forms with fancy; yet, to imagine
An Antony, were Nature's piece 'gainst fancy,
Condemning shadows quite.

THE DOVE

VENUS AND ADONIS

'Witness this primrose bank whereon I lie;
These forceless flowers like sturdy trees support
    me;
Two strengthless doves will draw me through
    the sky,
From morn till night, even where I list to sport
    me:
    Is love so light, sweet boy, and may it be
    That thou shouldst think it heavy unto thee?

'Is thine own heart to thine own face affected?
Can thy right hand seize love upon thy left?
Then woo thyself, be of thyself rejected,
Steal thine own freedom, and complain on
    theft.
    Narcissus so himself himself forsook,
    And died to kiss his shadow in the brook.'

The Dragon

KING HENRY VI, PART I

ACT I   SCENE I

Bedford:

Hung be the heavens with black, yield day to night!
Comets, importing change of times and states,
Brandish your crystal tresses in the sky;
And with them scourge the bad revolting stars,
That have concented unto Henry's death!
King Henry the fifth, too famous to live long!
England ne'er lost a king of so much worth.

Gloucester:

England ne'er had a king until his time.
Virtue he had, deserving to command:
His brandish'd sword did blind men with his beams;
His arms spread wider than a dragon's wings:
His sparkling eyes, replete with wrathful fire,
More dazzled and drove back his enemies,
Than mid-day sun, fierce bent against their faces.
What should I say? his deeds exceed all speech:
He ne'er lift up his hand but conquered.

THE DRAGON

THE EAGLE

KING HENRY V

ACT I   SCENE II

Westmoreland:

B ut there's a saying, very old and true, –

  If that you will France win,
  Then with Scotland first begin;

For once the eagle England being in prey,
To her unguarded nest the weasel Scot
Comes sneaking, and so sucks her princely eggs;
Playing the mouse, in absence of the cat,
To spoil and havoc more than she can eat.

Exeter:

It follows, then, the cat must stay at home:
Yet that is but a crush'd necessity;
Since we have locks to safeguard necessaries,
And pretty traps to catch the petty thieves,
While that the armed hand doth fight abroad,
The advisèd head defends itself at home:
For government, through high, and low, and lower,
Put into parts, doth keep in one concent;
Congreeing in a full and natural close,
Like music.

$\mathcal{T}$HE ELEPHANT

TROILUS AND CRESSIDA

ACT I   SCENE II

Alexander:

This man, lady, hath robbed many beasts of their particular additions; he is as valiant as the lion, churlish as the bear, slow as the elephant; a man into whom nature hath so crowded humours, that his valour is crushed into folly, his folly sauced with discretion: there is no man hath a virtue that he hath not a glimpse of; nor any man an attaint but he carries some stain of it: he is melancholy without cause, and merry against the hair: he hath the joints of everything, but everything so out of joint, that he is a gouty Briareus, many hands and no use; or purblinded Argus, all eyes and no sight.

Cressida:

But how should this man, that makes me smile, make Hector angry?

Alexander:

They say he yesterday coped Hector in the battle, and struck him down; the disdain and shame whereof hath ever since kept Hector fasting and waking.

CHE ELEPHANT

THE FOX

ACT V   SCENE III

Lear:

Upon such sacrifices, my Cordelia,
The gods themselves throw incense. Have I caught
    thee?
He that parts us shall bring a brand from heaven,
And fire us hence, like foxes. Wipe thine eyes;
The good years shall devour them, flesh and fell,
Ere they shall make us weep: we'll see them starve
    first.
Come.

THE FOX

KING HENRY IV, PART I

ACT V   SCENE II

Worcester:

Then are we all undone.
It is not possible, it cannot be,
The king would keep his word in loving us:
He will suspect us still, and find a time
To punish this offence in other faults:
Suspicion, all our lives, shall be stuck full of eyes:
For treason is but trusted like the fox;
Who, ne'er so tame, so cherish'd, and lock'd up,
Will have a wild trick of his ancestors.
Look how we can, or sad, or merrily,
Interpretation will misquote our looks;
And we shall feed like oxen at a stall,
The better cherish'd still the nearer death.
My nephew's trespass may be well forgot,
It hath the excuse of youth, and heat of blood;
And an adopted name of privilege, –
A hare-brain'd Hotspur, govern'd by a spleen:
All his offences live upon my head,
And on his father's; – we did train him on;
And, his corruption being ta'en from us,
We, as the spring of all, shall pay for all.
Therefore, good cousin, let not Harry know,
In any case, the offer of the king.

THE GOAT

OTHELLO

ACT III   SCENE III

Othello:

Think'st thou, I'd make a life of jealousy,
To follow still the changes of the moon
With fresh suspicions? No: to be once in doubt,
Is once to be resolved. Exchange me for a goat,
When I shall turn the business of my soul
To such exsufflicate and blown surmises,
Matching thy inference. 'Tis not to make me jealous,
To say my wife is fair, feeds well, loves company,
Is free of speech, sings, plays, and dances;
Where virtue is, these are more virtuous:
Nor from mine own weak merits will I draw
The smallest fear, or doubt of her revolt;
For she had eyes, and chose me. No, Iago;
I'll see before I doubt: when I doubt, prove;
And, on the proof, there is no more but this,-
Away at once with love, or jealousy.

THE GRIFFIN

KING HENRY IV, PART I

ACT III   SCENE I

Hotspur:

I cannot choose: sometime he angers me,
With telling me of the moldwarp and the ant,
Of the dreamer Merlin, and his prophecies;
And of a dragon and a finless fish,
A clip-wing'd griffin, and a moulten raven,
A couching lion, and a ramping cat,
And such a deal of skimble-skamble stuff
As puts me from my faith. I tell you what, –
He held me, last night, at least nine hours,
In reckoning up the several devils' names
That were his lackeys: I cried, *hum*, – and *well*, – *go to*, –
But mark'd him not a word. O, he's as tedious
As is a tired horse, a railing wife;
Worse than a smoky house: – I had rather live
With cheese and garlic in a windmill, far,
Than feed on cates, and have him talk to me,
In any summer-house in Christendom.

THE HART

ACT III   SCENE I

Antony:

That I did love thee, Caesar, O, 'tis true:
If then thy spirit look upon us now,
Shall it not grieve thee, dearer than thy death,
To see thy Antony making his peace,
Shaking the bloody fingers of thy foes,
Most noble! in the presence of thy corse?
Had I as many eyes as thou hast wounds,
Weeping as fast as they stream forth thy blood,
It would become me better, than to close
In terms of friendship with thine enemies.
Pardon me, Julius! – Here wast thou bay'd, brave hart;
Here didst thou fall; and here thy hunters stand,
Sign'd in thy spoil, and crimson'd in thy lethe.
O world! thou wast the forest to this hart;
And this, indeed, O world! the heart of thee. –
How like a deer, stricken by many princes,
Dost thou here lie!

THE HIND

AS YOU LIKE IT

ACT III   SCENE II

Touchstone:

If a hart do lack a hind,
Let him seek out Rosalind.
If the cat will after kind,
So, be sure, will Rosalind.
Winter-garments must be lined,
So must slender Rosalind.
They that reap must sheaf and bind;
Then to cart with Rosalind.
Sweetest nut hath sourest rind,
Such a nut is Rosalind.
He that sweetest rose will find,
Must find love's prick and Rosalind.

THE HORSE

VENUS AND ADONIS

His ears up prick'd; his braided hanging mane
Upon his compass'd crest now stand on end;
His nostrils drink the air, and forth again,
As from a furnace, vapours doth he send:
   His eye, which scornfully glisters like fire,
   Shows his hot courage and his high desire.

Sometimes he trots, as if he told the steps,
With gentle majesty, and modest pride;
Anon he rears upright, curvets, and leaps,
As who should say, Lo! thus my strength is tried;
   And this I do to captivate the eye
   Of the fair breeder that is standing by.

What recketh he his rider's angry stir,
His flattering 'holla,' or his 'Stand, I say'?
What cares he now for curb, or pricking spur?
For rich caparisons, or trapping gay?
   He sees his love, and nothing else he sees,
   Nor nothing else with his proud sight agrees.

Look, when a painter would surpass the life,
In limning out a well-proportion'd steed,
His art with nature's workmanship at strife,
As if the dead the living should exceed;
   So did this horse excel a common one,
   In shape, in courage, colour, pace, and bone.

THE HORSE

Round-hoof'd, short-jointed, fetlocks shag and long,
Broad breast, full eye, small head, and nostril wide,
High crest, short ears, straight legs, and passing
    strong,
Thin mane, thick tail, broad buttock, tender hide:
  Look, what a horse should have, he did not lack,
  Save a proud rider on so proud a back.

Sometime he scuds far off, and there he stares;
Anon he starts at stirring of a feather;
To bid the wind a base he now prepares,
And whether he run, or fly, they knew not whether;
  For through his mane and tail the high wind sings.
  Fanning the hairs, who wave like feather'd wings.

He looks upon his love, and neighs unto her;
She answers him, as if she knew his mind:
Being proud, as females are, to see him woo her,
She puts on outward strangeness, seems unkind;
  Spurns at his love, and scorns the heat he feels,
  Beating his kind embracements with her heels.

Then, like a melancholy malcontent,
He vails his tail, that, like a falling plume,
Cool shadow to his melting buttock lent;
He stamps, and bites the poor flies in his fume:
  His love, perceiving how he is enraged,
  Grew kinder, and his fury was assuaged.

ＣHE HORSE

THE HORSE

SONNET LI

Thus can my love excuse the slow offence
Of my dull bearer, when from thee I speed:
From where thou art why should I haste me thence?
Till I return, of posting is no need.
O, what excuse will my poor beast then find,
When swift extremity can seem but slow?
Then should I spur, though mounted on the wind;
In winged speed no motion shall I know:
Then can no horse with my desire keep pace;
Therefore desire, of perfect'st love being made,
Shall neigh (no dull flesh) in his fiery race;
But love, for love, thus shall excuse my jade, –
    Since from thee going he went wilful-slow,
    Towards thee I'll run, and give him leave to go.

THE LION

TIMON OF ATHENS

ACT IV   SCENE III

Timon:

If thou wert the lion, the fox would beguile thee; if thou wert the lamb, the fox would eat thee: if thou wert the fox, the lion would suspect thee, when, peradventure, thou wert accused by the ass: if thou wert the ass, thy dulness would torment thee; and still thou livedst but as a breakfast to the wolf: if thou wert the wolf, thy greediness would afflict thee, and oft thou shouldst hazard thy life for thy dinner: wert thou the unicorn, pride and wrath would confound thee, and make thine own self the conquest of thy fury: wert thou a bear, thou wouldst be killed by the horse; wert thou a horse, thou wouldst be seized by the leopard: wert thou a leopard, thou wert german to the lion, and the spots of thy kindred were jurors on thy life: all thy safety were remotion; and thy defence, absence. What beast couldst thou be, that were not subject to a beast? and what a beast art thou already, that see'st not thy loss in transformation!

THE LION

JULIUS CAESAR

ACT I   SCENE III

Cassius:

You look pale, and gaze,
And put on fear, and cast yourself in wonder,
To see the strange impatience of the heavens:
But if you would consider the true cause
Why all these fires, why all these gliding ghosts,
Why birds and beasts, from quality and kind;
Why old men, fools, and children calculate;
Why all these things change from their ordinance,
Their natures, and pre-formed faculties,
To monstrous quality; – why, you shall find,
That heaven hath infused them with these spirits,
To make them instruments of fear and warning
Unto some monstrous state.
Now could I, Casca, name to thee a man
Most like this dreadful night;
That thunders, lightens, opens graves, and roars
As doth the lion in the Capitol;
A man no mightier than thyself, or me,
In personal action; yet prodigious grown,
And fearful, as these strange eruptions are.

Casca:

'Tis Caesar that you mean: is it not, Cassius?

THE OWL

VENUS AND ADONIS

Look, the world's comforter, with weary gait,
His day's hot task hath ended in the west:
The owl, night's herald, shrieks – 'tis very late;
The sheep are gone to fold, birds to their nest;
    And coal-black clouds that shadow heaven's light
    Do summon us to part, and bid good night.

'Now let me say "good night," and so say you;
If you will say so, you shall have a kiss.'
'Good night,' quoth she; and, ere he says 'adieu,'
The honey fee of parting tender'd is:
    Her arms do lend his neck a sweet embrace;
    Incorporate then they seem; face grows to face;

Tilll, breathless, he disjoin'd, and backward drew
The heavenly moisture, that sweet coral mouth,
Whose precious taste her thirsty lips well knew,
Whereon they surfeit, yet complain on drouth:
    He with her plenty press'd, she faint with dearth,
    (Their lips together glued,) fall to the earth.

THE PANTHER

TITUS ANDRONICUS

ACT II   SCENE II

Titus Andronicus:

The hunt is up, the morn is bright and gray,
The fields are fragrant, and the woods are green;
Uncouple here, and let us make a bay,
And wake the emperor and his lovely bride,
And rouse the prince, and ring a hunter's peal,
That all the court may echo with the noise.
Sons, let it be your charge, as it is ours,
To attend the emperor's person carefully:
I have been troubled in my sleep this night,
But dawning day new comfort hath inspired . . .

Marcus:

I have dogs, my lord,
Will rouse the proudest panther in the chase,
And climb the highest promontory top.

Titus Andronicus:

And I have horse will follow where the game
Makes way, and run like swallows o'er the plain.

Demetrius:

Chiron, we hunt not, we, with horse nor hound;
But hope to pluck a dainty doe to ground.

THE PEACOCK

TROILUS AND CRESSIDA

ACT III   SCENE III

Thersites:

Why, he stalks up and down like a peacock, – a stride, and a stand: ruminates, like an hostess that hath no arithmetic but her brain to set down her reckoning: bites his lip with a politic regard, as who would say, – *there were wit in this head, an't would out*; and so there is; but it lies as coldly in him as fire in a flint, which will not show without knocking. The man's undone for ever; for if Hector break not his neck i' the combat, he'll break it himself in vain-glory. He knows not me: I said, *Good morrow, Ajax*; and he replies, *Thanks, Agamemnon*. What think you of this man, that takes me for the general? He is grown a very land-fish, languageless, a monster. A plague of opinion! a man may wear it on both sides, like a leather jerkin.

THE RABBIT

LOVE'S LABOUR'S LOST

ACT III   SCENE I

Moth:

Master, will you win your love with a French brawl?

Armado:

How meanest thou? brawling in French?

Moth:

No, my complete master: but to jig off a tune at the tongue's end, canary to it with your feet, humour it with turning up your eyelids; sigh a note, and sing a note; sometime through the throat, as if you swallowed love with singing love; sometime through the nose, as if you snuffed up love by smelling love; with your hat, penthouse-like, o'er the shop of your eyes; with your arms crossed on your thin belly-doublet, like a rabbit on a spit; or your hands in your pocket, like a man after the old painting; and keep not too long in one tune, but a snip and away. These are complements, these are humours; these betray nice wenches, that would be betrayed without these; and make them men of note, (do you note, men?) that most are affected to these.

THE RAM

THE MERCHANT OF VENICE

ACT I SCENE III

Shylock:

When Jacob grazed his uncle Laban's sheep,
This Jacob from our holy Abraham was
(As his wise mother wrought in his behalf)
The third possessor; ay, he was the third.

Antonio:

And what of him? did he take interest?

Shylock:

No, not take interest; not, as you would say,
Directly interest: mark what Jacob did.
When Laban and himself were compromised,
That all the eanlings which were streak'd and pied
Should fall, as Jacob's hire; the ewes, being rank,
In end of autumn turned to the rams:
And when the work of generation was
Between these woolly breeders in the act,
The skilful shepherd pill'd me certain wands,
And, in the doing of the deed of kind,
He stuck them up before the fulsome ewes;
Who, then conceiving, did in eaning-time
Fall particolour'd lambs, and those were Jacob's.
This was a way to thrive, and he was blest;
And thrift is blessing, if men steal it not.

THE RAM

ACT III   SCENE II

Corin:

Sir, I am a true labourer; I earn that I eat, get that I wear; owe no man hate, envy no man's happiness; glad of other men's good, content with my harm; and the greatest of my pride is, to see my ewes graze and my lambs suck.

Touchstone:

That is another simple sin in you; to bring the ewes and the rams together, and to offer to get your living by the copulation of cattle: to be bawd to a bell-wether; and to betray a she-lamb of a twelvemonth, to a crooked-pated, old, cuckoldly ram, out of all reasonable match. If thou be'st not damned for this, the devil himself will have no shepherds; I cannot see else how thou shouldst 'scape.

THE RAT

THE MERCHANT OF VENICE

ACT IV   SCENE I

Shylock:

What if my house be troubled with a rat,
And I be pleased to give ten thousand ducats
To have it baned? What, are you answer'd yet?
Some men there are love not a gaping pig;
Some, that are mad if they behold a cat;
And others, when the bagpipe sings i' the nose,
Cannot contain their urine: for affection,
Master of passion, sways it to the mood
Of what it likes, or loathes. Now, for your
  answer.
As there is no firm reason to be render'd,
Why he cannot abide a gaping pig;
Why he, a harmless necessary cat;
Why he, a woollen bagpipe, – but of force
Must yield to such inevitable shame,
As to offend, himself being offended;
So can I give no reason, nor I will not,
More than a lodged hate, and a certain loathing,
I bear Antonio, that I follow thus
A losing suit against him.

THE STAG

KING HENRY VI, PART I

ACT IV   SCENE II

French General:

Hark! hark! the Dauphin's drum, a warning bell,
Sings heavy music to thy timorous soul,
And mine shall ring thy dire departure out.

Talbot:

He fables not, I hear the enemy; —
Out, some light horsemen, and peruse their wings. —
O, negligent and heedless discipline!
How are we park'd, and bounded in a pale;
A little herd of England's timorous deer,
Mazed with a yelping kennel of French curs!
If we be English deer, be then in blood:
Not rascal-like, to fall down with a pinch;
But rather moody-mad and desperate stags,
Turn on the bloody hounds with heads of steel,
And make the cowards stand aloof at bay:
Sell every man his life as dear as mine,
And they shall find dear deer of us, my friends.
God, and saint George! Talbot, and England's right!
Prosper our colours in this dangerous fight!

THE STAG

THE MERRY WIVES OF WINDSOR

ACT V   SCENE V

Falstaff:

The Windsor bell hath struck twelve; the minute draws on: now the hot-blooded gods assist me! – Remember, Jove, thou wast a bull for thy Europa; love set on thy horns. O powerful love! that, in some respects, makes a beast a man; in some other, a man a beast. You were also, Jupiter, a swan, for the love of Leda: – O, omnipotent love! how near the god drew to the complexion of a goose! – A fault done first in the form of a beast; – O Jove, a beastly fault! and then another fault in the semblance of a fowl! think on't, Jove; a foul fault. When gods have hot backs, what shall poor men do? For me, I am here a Windsor stag; and the fattest, I think, i' the forest: send me a cool rut-time, Jove, or who can blame me to piss my tallow? Who comes here? my doe?

Mistress Ford:

Sir John? art thou there, my deer? my male deer?

Falstaff:

My doe with the black scut. Let the sky rain potatoes; let it thunder to the tune of *Green Sleeves*; hail kissing-comfits, and snow eringoes; let there come a tempest of provocation, I will shelter me here.

Mistress Ford:

Mistress Page is come with me, sweetheart.

Falstaff:

Divide me like a bribe-buck, each a haunch: I will keep my sides to myself, my shoulders for the fellow of this walk, and my horns I bequeath your husbands. Am I a woodman? ha! Speak I like Herne the hunter? – Why, now is Cupid a child of conscience: he makes restitution. As I am a true spirit, welcome!

THE TIGER

THE TWO GENTLEMEN OF VERONA

ACT III   SCENE II

Proteus:

S ay, that upon the altar of her beauty
You sacrifice your tears, your sighs, your heart:
Write till your ink be dry; and with your tears
Moist it again; and frame some feeling line,
That may discover such integrity:
For Orpheus' lute was strung with poets' sinews;
Whose golden touch could soften steel and stones,
Make tigers tame, and huge leviathans
Forsake unsounded deeps to dance on sands.
After your dire lamenting elegies,
Visit by night your lady's chamber-window,
With some sweet consort: to their instruments
Tune a deploring dump; the night's dead silence
Will well become such sweet complaining grievance.
This or else nothing, will inherit her.

Duke:

This discipline shows thou hast been in love.

Thurio:

And thy advice this night I'll put in practice.
Therefore, sweet Proteus, my direction-giver,
Let us into the city presently
To sort some gentlemen well-skill'd in music:
I have a sonnet that will serve the turn,
To give the onset to thy good advice.

THE TIGER

KING LEAR

ACT IV SCENE II

Albany:

Wisdom and goodness to the vile seem vile:
Filths savour but themselves. What have you
    done:
Tigers, not daughters, what have you perform'd?
A father, and a gracious agèd man,
Whose reverence even the head-lugg'd bear
    would lick, –
Most barbarous, most degenerate! – have you
    madded.
Could my good brother suffer you to do it?
A man, a prince, by him so benefited?
If that the heavens do not their visible spirits
Send quickly down to tame these vile offences,
'Twill come,
Humanity must perforce prey on itself,
Like monsters of the deep.

THE TOAD

ACT IV   SCENE III

Timon:

That nature, being sick of man's unkindness,
Should yet be hungry! – Common mother, thou,
Whose womb unmeasurable, and infinite breast,
Teems, and feeds all; whose self-same mettle,
Whereof thy proud child, arrogant man, is puff'd,
Engenders the black toad, and adder blue,
The gilded newt, and eyeless venom'd worm,
With all the abhorred births below crisp heaven
Whereon Hyperion's quickening fire doth shine;
Yield him, who all the human sons doth hate,
From forth thy plenteous bosom, one poor root!
Ensear thy fertile and conceptious womb,
Let it no more bring out ingrateful man!
Go great with tigers, dragons, wolves, and bears;
Teem with new monsters, whom thy upward face
Hath to the marbled mansion all above
Never presented! – O, a root, – dear thanks!
Dry up thy marrows, vines, and plough-torn leas;
Whereof ingrateful man, with liquorish draughts,
And morsels unctuous, greases his pure mind,
That from it all consideration slips!

124

THE TOAD

ACT II   SCENE I

Duke:

Sweet are the uses of adversity;
Which, like the toad, ugly and venomous,
Wears yet a precious jewel in his head;
And this our life, exempt from public haunt,
Finds tongues in trees, books in the running brooks,
Sermons in stones, and good in everything.
I would not change it.

Amiens:

Happy is your grace,
That can translate the stubbornness of fortune
Into so quiet and so sweet a style.

THE UNICORN

THE TEMPEST

ACT III   SCENE III

Sebastian:

Now I will believe
That there are unicorns; that in Arabia
There is one tree, the phoenix' throne; one phoenix
At this hour reigning there.

Antonio:

I'll believe both:
And what does else want credit, come to me,
And I'll be sworn 'tis true. Travellers ne'er did lie,
Though fools at home condemn them.

Gonzalo:

If in Naples
I should report this now, would they believe me?
If I should say I saw such islanders,
(For, certes, these are people of the island,)
Who, though they are of monstrous shape, yet,
    note,
Their manners are more gentle-kind, than of
Our human generation you shall find
Many, nay, almost any.

THE UNICORN

JULIUS CAESAR

ACT II   SCENE I

Decius:

Never fear that: if he be so resolved,
I can o'ersway him: for he loves to hear
That unicorns may be betray'd with trees,
And bears with glasses, elephants with holes,
Lions with toils, and men with flatterers:
But when I tell him he hates flatterers,
He says he does; being then most flatter'd.

PICTURE CREDITS

The animal illustrations (except for those
on pp.70, 71 and 74, from the Mary Evans
Picture Library) are taken from
MS Ashmole 1504, reproduced by courtesy of
the Bodleian Library, Oxford.